Hoodoo for Beginners

Hoodoo for Beginners

*Hoodoo Bible for Learning Herb and
Root Magic, Medicine, Oils, and Spells*

Mam Igbo

Legal Notice

Copyright 2022 Mam Igbo

The author offers information only.

No advice, health, legal, or otherwise, is offered in this book.

All rights are reserved.

This work may not be copied or disseminated in any form without written permission of the copyright holder.

Contents

Introduction 12

Chapter 1: Hoodoo History 14

Voodoo 16

The Role of Hoodoo in Modern Society 18

Chapter 2: Hoodoo Beliefs 20

Hoodoo Core Beliefs 20

Divine Providence 20

Death 21

Clairvoyance 22

The Doctrine of Signatures 22

Retributive Justice 23

Intention 24

The Book of Moses 25

Stars and Their Spiritual Meanings 26

Zodiac Signs and How They Affect
Intentions 27

The Morning and Evening Stars 30

Shooting Stars 30

Solomon's Pentagram 31

Chapter 3: Hoodoo Ingredients and
Materials 32

Goofer Dust 32

Graveyard Dirt 33

Plants and Herbs 34

   The Rose of Jericho 34

   Horsetail 35

   Basil 35

   John the Conqueror 35

   Palo Santo 36

   Cinnamon 36

Plants for Attracting Wealth 37

   The Money Plant 37

   The Mother-in-Law Plant 37

   Crassula 37

   Jasmine 38

   Bamboo 38

   Bayberry 38

   Chamomile 38

   Sage 39

Hoodoo Tools 39

   Amulets and Charms 39

   Coyote Claws 40

   Porcupine needles 40

Incense 41

Incense Blends and Their Uses: 41

Creating Your Formula 42

Various Hoodoo Tools 44

Chapter 4: Hoodoo Spiritual Cleansing 47

Things To Include in a Cleansing Kit 47

Personal Cleansing 48

Quick-Fix Methods 50

Cleansing and Blessing the Home 51

Cleansing Spells to Eliminate Toxicity ..55

Chapter 5: Hoodoo Mojo Bag 58

How to Make Your Mojo Bag 61

How Long Does a Mojo Bag Retain Its Power? 64

Chapter 6: Conjure Work 67

The Right Time to Perform Conjuring 68

Charging Your Lucky Talisman 69

The Powder of Powders 70

Oils 75

Other Types of Conjuring 78

Enhancing Your Conjure Work 80

Important Psalms Use for Strengthening Conjure Work.............81

Chapter 7: The Use of Candle Magic.......83

The Meaning of Candle Colors.............84

Hoodoo Candle Terminology.................86

Figure Candles.....................................88

How to Read Candle Burning...............90

The Meaning Behind Candle Flames....91

How to Read Candle Wax.....................93

How to Read Wax Puddles...................94

Chapter 8: Rootwork.................................96

Popular Roots and Herbs in Hoodoo....97

Creating Talismans and Amulets Using Herbs and Roots.................................102

How to Create an Amulet.................103

How to Create a Talisman...............104

How To Use Roots and Magic Herbs in Spell Work...106

Chapter 9: Hoodoo Divination................107

The Meaning Behind the Cards.......108

The Suits...108

The Individual Cards.......................109

How to Shuffle Your Deck...................113

Types of Birds and Their Meaning ..115

Observing Birds and Reading Flight
Patterns 117

Cleromancy 117

Curing Bones 118

Using The Bones 118

Oneiromancy.....................................119

Chapter 10: Hoodoo Spells for Love and
Luck 122

Luck Spells.......................................127

Setting Up Your Altar 127

Conclusion 135

An Introduction to Hoodoo

Introduction

Hoodoo has been around since the first Africans came to America as slaves and spread throughout the country, bringing with them their spiritual practices. Their core beliefs and the materials they used, including roots and herbs, were fused with other beliefs and practices. This has resulted in the formation of Hoodoo.

While it's easy to think that Hoodoo is just another form of spiritual practice, the truth is that Hoodoo is far from being one. The principles of Hoodoo aren't founded on the worship of god or goddess. Instead, Hoodoo is a way for people to practice folk magic with the use of certain ingredients and materials.

Perhaps you're wondering whether Hoodoo is still relevant in today's society. As a matter of fact, it is. While most of us may have forgotten the true power that lies within nature, many of us have rediscovered them and their uses.

Our ancestors have used magic and rootworking rituals in centuries past, and it's inevitable for what they have learned to be passed on to us. The thing about Hoodoo is that it can be practiced by anyone who wishes to try it. The key is to understand how the power works and learn to respect it.

This book will serve as a guide to the basics of Hoodoo and will provide everything you need to know about this practice so you too can use it in your daily life.

Chapter 1: Hoodoo History

Hoodoo originated during the time when African slaves were first brought to the shores of America. The African slaves developed it as a means of retaining their roots. As a folk magic, Hoodoo incorporates the systematic beliefs of ancient African cultures to that of Christianity, which was taught to the slaves by their slave masters.

While Hoodoo is not fundamentally a religion, it does present a set of deities that practitioners have the freedom to worship or not. It is believed that Hoodoo was developed as a means of protecting black people against oppression and should therefore only be used by black people.

Modern practitioners believe otherwise, claiming that Hoodoo has three different streams encompassing a person's race or ethnicity. First, there is the Black thread, which is meant for black people. Then, there's the White thread for people of

European influences. And finally, there's the Red thread, which is for Native Americans.

As a personal practice, Hoodoo is meant to be used in varying methods by different people. In that sense, Hoodoo can be influenced by a person's cultural and theological preferences. A core part of Hoodoo is ancestor veneration as it is founded on historical practices.

Hoodoo has no barriers. Practitioners can use it either to harm or to protect. The rituals involved are highly influenced by the intention of the person performing them. Essential to the practice is a knowledge of plants and herbs and the power they bear, as they can be used in conjunction with other magical elements.

The origin of the word "hoodoo" is widely disputed, although it is generally believed to have originated with the arrival of African slaves to America in the 17th century. While the slaves were allowed to practice folk magic, the extent to which they used it depended on their slave owner's tolerance.

Voodoo

Hoodoo is sometimes confused with Voodoo, but the main difference between the two is that Voodoo is a religion. Voodoo has practices not found in Hoodoo, and it has religious leaders that are required to go through ordination before they can practice. Hoodoo doesn't have such formality.

Voodoo also has two specific branches: Haitian Voodoo and Louisiana Voodoo (also known as New Orleans Voodoo). Haitian Voodoo is a religion in Africa that spread from Haiti. They have spirits called Lwa, which was a focal point that members of the religion relied on for guidance.

Louisiana Voodoo, on the other hand, relied upon the fusion of religious practices and deep spiritual roots, some of which are shared with Hoodoo. This branch of Voodoo blends the traditional Lwa spirits with Catholic symbolisms and saints. It uses English and French Creole as its liturgical language.

Both Haitian and Louisiana Voodoo use religious symbols called "veves" and other symbols for decorating their surroundings and use sand and cornmeal to draw them on the ground. All symbols used by these two branches have meanings. The veves are meant to create a connection between the physical and spiritual worlds. When used in rituals, the participants invite Lwa spirits to possess their bodies to use for transportation.

Unfortunately, Voodoo has gained a bad reputation when the media started to portray it inaccurately with Voodoo dolls that were used to harm people and spell casting to turn dead people into zombies. In reality, there are no such things in Voodoo or Hoodoo. Both practices do not rely on Satan or demons at all. The use of magic dolls to harm others is a form of European witchcraft and is not practiced in either Voodoo or Hoodoo.

The main aim of Hoodoo as a Southern folk magic is to heal and to help improve certain aspects of a person's life. This is why Hoodoo relies hugely on magical baths and powders, as well as lamps and candles used to perform spells. You may be surprised to learn that these rituals are also accompanied by readings and prayers from the Bible and the invoking of Catholic saints.

The Role of Hoodoo in Modern Society

Our society today is becoming more open to the exploration of spiritualism, and that includes hoodoo. One reason is that we now have the means in the form of technology to study different cultures and explore their beliefs and teachings. For instance, we've long been interested in shamanism and witchcraft. Norse religions and Wicca have also risen in popularity these days, and now, our interest is in Hoodoo.

What's great about Hoodoo is that it allows practitioners of this age to embrace elements from various parts of the world and blend them with influences coming from other cultures. Classes can be taken online, and practitioners now have access to forces to help them improve certain areas of their lives, be it romance, career, or health. Some also learn to cast spells to get revenge against those who have harmed them.

The number one thing you need to understand when learning Hoodoo, however, is that you have to respect its history and learn to appreciate its foundations. Hoodoo was associated with some violence in the past, but that can change. You can use Hoodoo instead to improve your life and create a meaningful impact in the lives of those around you.

People like Harry Hyatt and Zora Hurston were integral to the revival of belief and practice of Hoodoo. They worked hard to preserve the practices of Hoodoo, which is the reason for it starting to grow into popularity again.

Chapter 2: Hoodoo Beliefs

Hoodoo embraces an extensive range of beliefs that allow its followers to adopt teachings from other cultures. It's not bound by a certain set of rules, and practitioners are free to choose which form of Hoodooism to practice.

Many of the core beliefs of Hoodoo are easy to recognize in today's society. Such beliefs give practitioners a core belief system rather than limit them. Practitioners have the freedom to choose which higher being they want to follow and are not judged or condemned regardless of who they choose to call on.

Hoodoo Core Beliefs

Divine Providence

The first thing that comes to mind when "Divine Providence" is mentioned is God.

That's because conventional theism is founded on one central figure that has control of the entire cosmos. Such belief teaches that there is one higher being who is responsible for everything that exists. Hoodoo, however, doesn't require practitioners to follow one god and one god alone.

With Hoodoo, it's not unusual for practitioners to incorporate multiple gods into their belief system as long as those gods meet their needs. For instance, they can call on Jesus for healing or protection and appeal to Santa Muertos to help them find a romantic partner.

Death

For rootworkers, death is not the end. In fact, it is part of their practice to call on their ancestors to guide them in their daily lives. Practitioners of Hoodoo believe that when the physical body passes, the soul ascends to a higher realm to become an ancestor. Living relatives can then consult them when needing advice. Ancestors also intercede with higher spirits on the behalf of their living relatives.

Clairvoyance

One of the most powerful tools in the bag of a conjurer doctor is the power of sight. Practitioners who are able to see the future and communicate with spirits have a higher status in the community. With this power, practitioners can travel freely between the past and the present to find the best solution to a present dilemma. Divination allows them to take part in the lives of other people to help turn their situation around.

The Doctrine of Signatures

Hoodoo practices the doctrine of signatures, teaching that plants display characteristics indicative of the diseases they can treat and cure. Hoodoo teaches that there is a cosmic signature on every object in the universe that indicates its purpose or intended use.

Walnuts, for instance, have an appearance similar to that of the human brain. Healers in the past believed that these seeds were effective for treating ailments related to the head. Today, scientists tell us walnuts are rich in fatty acids that help improve memory function.

Stinging nettles, on the other hand, have hairs similar to those in human heads. Traditional healers use them as cream or lotion to help improve blood circulation, which in turn, helps grow hair on bald people. At the same time, the hairs look like animal stings, making them an effective treatment against insect stings and bites.

Finally, there's lungwort, a plant with white spots resembling the marks on sick lungs. As a result, this plant is used to treat lung problems, such as tuberculosis, coughs, and asthma.

Retributive Justice

Hoodoo is practiced mainly for improving the lives of human beings. Most religions and philosophy teach the importance of treating others with kindness and doing no harm to one's fellow. With Hoodoo, however, there is the principle of an "eye for an eye," which was taken directly from the Bible. Hoodoo believes that people have the right to demand for justice. This is why

Hoodoo allows its followers to practice retributive justice in the form of inflicting harm on oppressors through an illness or other forms of pain.

Intention

Some Hoodoo belief systems hold that a power exists for cursing others. Practitioners believe that these jinxes and hexes will only work if the person they are intended for is deserving of the curse. Followers usually have powders that are labeled with intentions. For instance, there's the Boss Fix, a powder designed to hex your boss to put them in their place.

There's also the Confusion Powder, designed to confuse individuals who go against you with bad intentions. The Court Case Powder, on the other hand, is used to influence the judge and jury in the court. Meanwhile, the Hotfoot Sachets are used to drive people away from your life, while the Devil's Shoestring Sachet is used for restraining enemies.

Again, these jinxes only work if the people they are for truly deserve the hex. The Boss Fix powder, for instance, will only work on a boss within a workplace and won't affect other employees. Most importantly, it will only work against a cruel boss.

In short, nobody will receive a curse without a reason. This belief is based on the Bible, particularly Proverbs 26:2, which states that "an undeserved curse will not come to rest."

The Book of Moses

A lesser-known influence of Hoodoo is the "Sixth and Seventh Book of Moses." This book contains over 125 articles that a Hoodoo follower can use in magical practices. Hex Signs listed in the book are powerful symbols and talismans used to protect one against very powerful curses. They can be painted on household furniture and objects to protect people who own them.

According to legend, it was God who dictated the detailed witchcraft guide to Moses in Mount Sinai, but it was not included in the Old Testament considering its power. Nevertheless, the contents of the book reached King Solomon, who used the guide to later on become one of the most powerful and prominent figures in the Christian religion.

Stars and Their Spiritual Meanings

The heavenly bodies remain a mystery to this day even with the knowledge and technology that we now have. Since ancient times, the night skies have been a source of wonder and fascination. One can only imagine how they appealed to our ancestors, particularly the African slaves who were bound by chains and stripped off their freedom.

Unsurprisingly, Hoodoo gets much of its influence from the stars, much like many religions, spiritual, and mythological systems. We all know this as astrology. The term "astrology" comes from the Greek words "Astron," meaning "a star," and "logos," meaning "that is said." This suggests that the stars actually contain God's word.

It's worth noting that astrology is not an orthodox Hoodoo technique. The signs of the Zodiac, plus the phases of the moon, were often used to affect the timing of spells.

Zodiac Signs and How They Affect Intentions

Aries: The house of self. The new moon period in Aries means changing one's self and methods.

Taurus: The house of money. This is the time for setting intentions regarding money and wealth.

Gemini: The house of travel. This is the perfect sign of starting new journeys. Setting your intentions during this period will increase your success.

Cancer: The house of family. Setting intentions when the moon is cancer will help form stronger family bonds.

Leo: The house of love. The moon being in Leo is the perfect time to attract a romantic partner. It also increases the chances of a couple conceiving a child.

Virgo: The house of work. Intentions regarding work and career are favorable during this period. This is also the best time to start a new health routine, such as a new diet or exercise program.

Libra: The house of relationships. The new moon being in the house of Libra signals that it's the time to work on your social connections.

Scorpio: The house of enigma. When the moon is in the house of Scorpio, it's the best time for you to set intentions regarding shared resources. This includes resolving tax issues and paying off debt.

Sagittarius: The house of knowledge. Intentions surrounding the expansion of horizons and embracing new subjects is most auspicious. This is the best time to plan for a new trip or for taking an online course about a subject you're not familiar with.

Capricorn: The house of public. The best time to work on your public image is when the moon aligns with the house of Capricorn. This could mean updating your online presence or your CV.

Aquarius: The house of friendship. This is the best time to set intentions to either strengthen existing friendships or meet new people.

Pisces: The house of the hidden. This is the perfect time to discover your inner self. Set intentions to improve yourself and cease focusing on other people for a while.

Hoodoo oils play a significant role in astrological timings. Certain oils can increase the effectiveness of the moon's phases on the person using the oil. In addition, astral signs are also an important part of Hoodoo teachings. Hoodoo followers use stars as guides. Stars represent divine energy, and practitioners direct their intentions toward specific heavenly bodies depending on their goals.

The Morning and Evening Stars

The Morning and Evening Stars refer to a single celestial body. It only has two names because it appears at different times, and people used to think the two are different stars.

The Morning Star leads the sun into the sunrise. It is a leading light that carries with it knowledge and power. When the sun sets, the Morning Star can be seen shining brightly beside the sun before disappearing with it on the horizon.

There's a belief that the star is an embodiment of Lucifer, whose name means "bringer of light."

Shooting Stars

Shooting stars are interpreted in various ways depending on the culture. Some believe that one can bring good fortune, a positive omen. Others believe it's a fallen angel. In Asian cultures, shooting stars are a bad omen. Followers of Hoodoo interpret

the meaning depending on which culture
they belong to.

Solomon's Pentagram

Solomon's pentagram is often associated
with dark magic. Historically speaking, the
opposite is true. Hoodoo practitioners have
used this symbol from the very beginning to
set intentions for generations. Various
combinations exist, some promoting love,
wealth, and blessings, while others
punishing immoral acts. As the ultimate sign
of wisdom and power, Solomon's
pentagram is often combined with other
pentacle symbols.

Chapter 3: Hoodoo Ingredients and Materials

Hoodoo spells and practices include dust and dirt. That's because these elements are readily available to the first people who practiced Hoodoo. The Goofer dust, in particular, is one of the most important magic components of Hoodoo.

Goofer Dust

The term 'Goofer' is derived from the Bantu word 'kufua,' which means "to die." It is used to either harm or kill the targeted individual. Goofer dust is composed mainly of graveyard dirt and dust, although it may also contain other ingredients depending on the outcome desired. Two common elements added are snakeskin and salt. These are both used to create a powerful way to cause harm to the target victim.

The dust is spread on the pillow of the victim or around the victim's path. The hex works by first causing sharp pains in the legs and feet of the target. The legs will then swell so that the victim is unable to walk.

Over time, the practice has evolved to become an expression known as "goofering someone," which is the act of inflicting harm by spreading injurious elements around the victim's environment.

Graveyard Dirt

The Bokongo people who came from Central Africa were believed to have first used graveyard dirt in their magic. They believed that graveyard dirt contained the spirits of dead people. This type of dirt cannot just be taken, though, but needs to be bought. This means the practitioner must commune with the dead person and create a contract first. This usually involves leaving gifts on the grave of the deceased in the form of something the deceased used to enjoy, such as liquor, food, or various objects.

Not all graveyard dirts possess equal power. Dirt from the graves of young children and infants are thought to be especially powerful for bringing healing and good fortune. Meanwhile, dirt acquired from above the heart is often used for love spells.

Plants and Herbs

Plants and herbs play a major role in Hoodoo. Here's a list of some of the most common ones used for Hoodoo magic.

The Rose of Jericho

Also known as the resurrection plant or the false plant, the Rose of Jericho originated from Mexico. It's brown and very brittle when dry. However, when immersed in water, it spreads out and becomes vibrant. It transforms into a sacred plant with perfect symmetry. As the name of the plant suggests, it is used to cast spells for resurrecting an old romance or creating a new one.

Horsetail

Horsetail is a verdant plant that usually grows in humid environments. It is known for its medicinal and magical properties. When correctly harvested, it can be used as antifungal. When harvested at the wrong time, it can be toxic.

Basil

Basil is used in Hoodoo to attract good fortune. It can create a powerful spell to attract love or induce prosperity. It can also be used to ward off bad vibes and evil spirits.

John the Conqueror

John the Conqueror is the name of a root medicine with powers that can be traced back to early African American folklore. A practitioner only needs to possess it to benefit from its powers that are associated with love and fortune. When you carry it with the hair of someone you are attracted to, that person will soon show admiration and interest in you as well.

Palo Santo

Palo Santo is considered in Hoodoo as one of the most sacred and powerful plants on the planet. It is found in South America and is used by Shamans and healers. It can be used to make herbal teas for cleansing the body and boosting the immune system.

Cinnamon

Cinnamon is readily available and is a very common part of a Hoodoo tool kit. It is used for sexual arousal spells, and when burned during sexual intercourse, it is said to help enhance the experience. Furthermore, cinnamon is used to attract wealth and prosperity.

Plants for Attracting Wealth

Many Hoodoo practices revolve around the attraction of money. For that reason, many of the plants used in Hoodoo are those that have power to do so.

The Money Plant

Also referred to as the golden pothos, the money plant is placed around sharp angles within the house to transform it into a place of success.

The Mother-in-Law Plant

This is also known as the snake plant. It is a healthy plant that provides a natural source of cleanliness and moisture.

Crassula

Crassula have succulent leaves and are used in Hoodoo to bring an abundance of finances to the home. The plant should be placed in the southeast corner for it to become effective.

Jasmine

This aromatic plant is used to attract money and good luck. It is also used as an aphrodisiac.

Bamboo

For centuries, bamboo has been believed to bring good luck and good health, especially in Asian cultures. Hoodoo embraces this idea and uses bamboo for the same reason. Lucky bamboo, in particular, is used to bring blessings to the home.

Bayberry

This shrub is grown in eastern part of the United States. When dried and blended, it can be used to attract prosperity and romance.

Chamomile

Chamomile is used for its healing and calming effects. Hoodoo followers used this daisy-like plant to bring wealth and influence.

Sage is well-known to be a powerful plant that cleanses and reinvigorates. In Hoodoo, it is used not only for its healing powers, but also for its ability to attract luck and love.

Hoodoo Tools

Hoodoo tools serve solely as a medium to direct the power that lies within the practitioner. They don't have magical powers in themselves and won't work apart from the spiritual intent of the one who uses them. Some users only need the barest essentials, while others will look for the most powerful tools available. This will depend on their intent.

Amulets and Charms

These items produce energies and vibrations for the user and the recipient. While they may seem like common tools, they can be very magical when placed in the right hands. It's important for users to have candles and holders, too, since they play an important role in certain rituals.

In most cases, the most effective amulets are the ones that have been formed by the user themselves. They contain personal effects, such as nail clippings or hair strands that provide them extra power.

Coyote Claws

Coyotes are animals known for their cunning ways. Despite the reputation of this wild dog, the coyote is believed to only have the best interest of man at its heart. Coyotes can travel in the dark and find resources in the most desolate places. Their claws are often carried by practitioners who want to stay concealed when traveling.

Porcupine needles

Porcupine needles can be used with dolls, rootwork, and candles. They can offer protection and are often placed around objects that need to be guarded.

Incense

Practitioners burn incense when performing rituals and spells. Doing so can enhance the experience. Clay bowls are usually used for burning incense with self-igniting charcoal as the source of fuel.

Incense Blends and Their Uses:

African juju - used to draw intense desire and passion into a romantic relationship
Seven African Powers - an orisha essence used for obtaining energy from the seven saints of Africa.
Banishing - used to remove harmful people from one's life.
Tranquility - an incense burned to bring peace and harmony to the home.
Chuparosa - known as the hummingbird incense, chuparosa is used to draw a lover closer
Has no Hanna - an incense used to enhance Hoodoo tools.
Obeah - this incense is burned to allow rootworkers and sorcerers to communicate with spirits.

Jinx killer - this is a special blend of incense that is burned to provide protection from all curses and hexes.

Dragon's blood - said to contain real dragon blood, this resin is burned to bring power when performing rituals.

There are companies creating and blending incense such as these. They also blend formula upon request.

Creating Your Formula

Creating your own formula is sometimes necessary to create powerful rootwork. You can combine herbs and other ingredients to do this. You can also purchase oils and powders that are ready-made.

Black Arts Oil

One of the most powerful Hoodoo blends, Black Arts Oil is used to cross up enemies who have caused harm to you or people you love. This oil can be created by using baneful substances, such as red pepper, snakeskin, and sulfur, which are then mixed with herbs of your choice.

Boss Fix Oil

Boss Fix Oil is a concoction developed to put people in authority in their right place. This oil is often placed on certain objects, so that when a boss touches them, they will experience discomfort or pain. Such a mixture can contain high john herbs, licorice, and other herbs, and is perfect for bosses who oppress their employees.

Poppets

Poppets are traditional dolls formed from wax or cloth and represent a spirit that is connected to the owner. There is a misconception that poppets are similar to voodoo dolls, but poppets are not intended for bringing harm. When making a poppet, the color of the cloth used will determine the power it will possess. Here's a list of powers and the color that represent them:

Banishing - Black fabric decorated with fire or swords.
Healing - White or blue with cloud and star decorations.

Ingenuity - Yellow or orange fabrics with fire or sun symbols.
Love and passion - Deep pink or red fabric with hearts and bows
Protection - White or red fabric with key or shield decorations.
Wealth - Gold or silver fabric with green trims.

Various Hoodoo Tools

Lodestones

These are naturally occurring magnetized stones used to draw positive influence. They are used to attract money and love and can direct spells from other users.

Lucky Blue Balls

Also known as anil, these balls made from copper sulfate are carried for good fortune. They are dissolved in water in some cases to provide a cleansing solution.

Pyrite

Also known as fool's good, pyrite is a shiny material commonly used to draw money and success to the user.

Coins

Certain types of coins are used in Hoodoo, most of which are for bringing luck to people who are suffering. They have no monetary value and are often sold in traditional shops.

Mojo Beans

Mojo beans are also called wishing beans. They are classic good luck charms and are supposed to be carried inside a red container to bring good fortune to the holder.

Twice Stricken Lightning Wood

This is actually powder ground from wood that has been struck twice by lightning. The powder has the power to attract and is used for sexual spells.

Bones

Throwing bones is a traditional form of divination in Hoodoo. The bones and how they are thrown will have meanings depending on the intention of the caster.

Chapter 4: Hoodoo Spiritual Cleansing

The Hoodoo toolkit is the most important part of practical Hoodoo work. As such, the materials must be kept physically clean. More importantly, the practitioner must be spiritually clean at all times. The ingredients used for cleansing will differ depending on the method and requirements of the practitioner, although there are standard components involved.

Spiritual cleansing is crucial for various reasons. One, it allows the practitioner to perform at their best. It also eliminates negative energies that may attach themselves to the practitioner and the environment.

Things To Include in a Cleansing Kit

- Candles
- Brick Dust

- Salt
- Chicken or Turkey wing
- Chicken foot
- Graveyard Dirt
- Crystals
- Holy Water
- Essential oils
- Alcohol Rub
- Natural bath salts
- Herbs, such as rosemary, sage, palo santo, and sweetgrass

Personal Cleansing

Personal cleansing is important especially during times that you're feeling anxious or ill. There will definitely be times that you will feel your powers are waning or that there are blockages in your aura. This is the perfect time for you to perform cleansing of your body and soul to help restore your power and energy levels.

Performing this act during certain planetary hours can make it more effective. It can increase the power of your ritual. Ritual baths are especially effective at cleansing the aura, so that you feel your power even hours after.

If you want to get rid of negative energies, perform a hot bath with natural bath salts, essential oil, 2 cups of blessed water, and a sprinkle of your favorite herbs. Place two white candles at the side of your bath area and light them up. Add all the ingredients to your bath to energize the atmosphere. Step in once the bath is filled.

Next, take a small container and pour the water over your head thirteen times. Do this while reciting a cleansing prayer. A common prayer option is Psalm 37, although you can also compose your own prayer. Wash downward only so that negative energies are washed into the bathwater.

Once you feel cleansed and refreshed, you can step out of the bath and airdry yourself. Be careful not to use any towels. Take a container full of the bathwater next and take it to a crossroads. Throw the water away over your shoulder and return home without looking back.

Quick-Fix Methods

There are alternative methods you can try if you can't use a bath to cleanse yourself due to time constraints.

The Chicken Foot - Lightly scratching yourself with a chicken foot will help remove negative energies from you. Like a chicken, you can scratch away the mess and move on.

Brushing - If you believe you need a more rigorous cleansing, then use a chicken or turkey wing instead. Take the turkey wing and brush it on the top of your head going down to the sole of your feet. This is a method for removing a jinx.

Rubdown - This includes using alcohol as a base. Infuse the mixture by adding some oil and herbs before rubbing it on yourself. Enhance the experience by performing the ritual in a sacred place and using prayers and chants.

Candle - You can use a black candle to get rid of a jinxed condition. Wipe yourself with the black candle in downward motions while saying a prayer.

Smoke - Using smoke for cleansing is called smudging. It can be performed by burning dried herbs, essential oils, or incense. Cover yourself with white cloth from the neck down and burn the item you prefer. Allow the smoke to circulate around you and remove the sheet to allow it to permeate the room.

Sprinkle - A sprinkler head can also be used for cleansing. Fill one with blessed or holy water mixed with essential oils or salt. Wet your head and shoulders while reciting your favorite. Sprinkle your feet last.

Cleansing and Blessing the Home

Floor washes that are based on the items used in personal cleansing can be used for cleaning the house and other places. The rules of washing are the same, making sure water is directed downward to carry all negative energies toward the ground and dispel bad luck. Prayers, smudging, and candles can be used for a deeper cleansing.

Practitioners often use elemental ingredients for increasing the power of the cleansing and blessing.

Earth

The most basic element form of Earth is dirt from the ground. If you don't want to use actual dirt, there are alternatives you can use instead.

Redbrick dust - This form of Earth is believed to be effective and is often sprinkled everywhere, including doorways, windows, entrances, and thresholds. The most powerful form is usually found in sacred buildings and old houses.

To form psychic barriers that are impenetrable, lay unbroken lines across your prosperity's thresholds. Perform this ritual during the eve of a full moon for a more powerful effect. Also, be sure to replace the dust every month.

Salt - Salt is a common element since it's readily available. It's also easy to remove. Sea salt is especially effective and is often used when dealing with bad dreams and nightmares. To get rid of sleep issues, sprinkle the area around the bed with sea salt or regular salt. Placing a container filled with salt at the front door will also help protect the home from negative energies.

Black Salt - This salt is a mixture of sea salt and regular salt, plus charcoal and iron filling. This is used when dealing with particularly strong negative energies.

Air

Air is an element that is naturally incorporated in house cleanses and blessings. It can be utilized by burning incense and candles with the doors and windows opened to let negative energies escape.

Fire

White and black candles are used to bring power to house cleanses. Their strength is increased by combining them with essential oils, such as Sandalwood or Myrrh.

Water

Deep cleanses of houses are based around this element. It can be used to wash away illnesses. Today, you can acquire blessed water by purchasing them in stores that sell Hoodoo items.

You can also bless your own water using the following method:

Step 1: Collect just enough seawater to use for your cleanse. Be sure to leave a gift for the spirits dwelling in the body of water from where you collected it.

Step 2: Collect rainwater. The best rainwater to use is one gathered during a thunderstorm,

Step 3: Leave the water you've collected overnight under the moonlight. Mix the seawater and rainwater in a glass container. Place the container on a table outside where it will receive the most moonlight exposure. Charge it with your prayers and blessings before leaving it overnight.

Step 4: Add salt to your water. Holy salt is ideal. Stir the water in a clockwise direction while adding the salt and say a prayer.

Cleansing Spells to Eliminate Toxicity

The world we live in is full of negative energy, which is why it's important to clear specific areas of negativity and frustrations. The following spells are designed specifically to focus on intentions rather than a general cleansing ritual.

Moonlight Spell

For this spell, you will need a white candle, an incense, and some calming music.

To perform, first, take a cleansing bath on the evening of a full moon and dress in a white robe after air-drying yourself.

Find a quiet place outdoors or by the window where you can directly see the moon.

Play some calming music and light your incense.

Call upon your spirit guide and ask them to protect your soul's energy and fill you with healing powers.

Feel the energy as it flows into you from the sole of your feet to the top of your head.

Around this time, begin forgiving yourself for your shortcomings and feel the pressures of the world to overcome you.

Finally, thank the cosmos for the blessings it has been providing you, and thank your spirit or angel for their help.

Spell for the Soul

Whenever you feel that your soul is heavy and burdened, you can regain control with the help of this spell. You will a white candle, holy salt, dried sage, blessed water, and a bowl for burning herbs.

Select a night of a waning moon to perform this spell. Light the candle first and invite the spirits to bless your ritual. Move your hand quickly through the flame of the candle and recite, "I use this fire to release negative energies within, and I ask that they be replaced with good intentions."

Next, rub the holy salt into your palms and recite, "Through this element, I relinquish all negative elements in my life."

After that, burn the dried sage in the bowl and breathe in the smoke and recite, "With the element of air, I cleanse my soul and eliminate all thoughts that trouble me."

Plunge both of your hands into the water and recite, "I use water to release toxins from within and bring clear and positive intentions to my soul."

And now, the ritual is done. Dispose of all the ingredients you used by mixing the salt with the ashes. Dissolve them in the water and scatter it at a crossroads or bury it under a tree.

Chapter 5: Hoodoo Mojo Bag

Using a mojo bag is one of the easiest ways to improve your magic practices and make them personally charged. Mojo bags are also called toby, conjuring sacks, condition bags, and gris-gris. There is no limit as to how many mojo bags you'd like to have. You can also tailor them to suit your needs and preferences.

Mojo bags are like batteries that keep your powers charged. That means you need to carry them with you always. Commercial bags are available, but a handmade bag will help you to better connect to your magical sources.

Color plays a major role when choosing a fabric for your mojo bag. For some, satin and rich velvets are the common options, while for others, it's cotton or muslin.

Silver - This color works with the moon. It's linked to the goddess yin who promotes peace and meditation.

Gold - Gold aligns with the sun and helps to attract wealth and success. The god yang is often associated with gold, providing a loud and bold type of energy.

Red - Red is connected to Mars and represents courage and passion. The deeper the shade of red, the more energetic the mojo will be.

Violet - Violet represents healing. It also aids in karmic connections. When you use this color, your tools will have power when you're using divine connections or connecting to the spirit world.

Orange - This color is linked to Mercury and represents success. It provides all the ingredients inside the bag with vitality and speed.

Blue - Blue is associated with Jupiter. Use this color for your bag if you want to bring wisdom to your spells.

Yellow - Yellow is governed by the sun and represents creativity and joy. It helps bring an aura of appeal to your spells.

Green - Green works with Venus and imbues your bag with wealth and good fortune.

Rose Pink - The color of love and friendship, rose pink is used to enhance creative and romantic skills.

Grey - Tools inside a grey mojo bag will have power for creating illusions. They will be effective when used for secretive moves and spells involving invisibility.

White - White is the color of spirituality and divination. A bag with this color will help you connect to angels. It will also help improve your psychological health.

Black - Black enhances the power of banishing spells. Associated with Saturn, black provides a level of discipline to the practitioner.

How to Make Your Mojo Bag

Step 1: Measure your fabric and cut it to form a rectangle that's three times as wide as it is long. For example, if you want to make it 12 inches long, make it 4 inches wide.

Step 2: Fold the cloth in half so that the rough side is facing outside and the smooth side facing inside. Position the ends and edges next and trim any excess strand.

Step 3: Sew the sides, leaving the last two inches untouched for the pocket. The top will serve as the opening, so leave it unsown.

Step 4: Turn the bag inside out, so that the smooth side is now facing outside. Fold the unsown fabric down to form a flap on each side of the bag.

Step 5: Using a pair of scissors, make four small incisions along the fold that you have just created.

Step 6: Thread a small ribbon or colored string through the slits, making sure it's long enough to cover the neck of the bag with excess for tying.

Step 7: Charge your bag by placing stones, herbs, crystals, and other elements to make it fit the purpose it was made for.

Step 8: Draw the string of the bag tight to keep the items safe and secure. This time, you will need to choose which objects you're going to keep in your mojo bag. The items will depend on your goal. Traditionally, mojo bags contain an odd number of items since odd numbers are considered dynamic and active. Moreover, the number of items should not exceed 13, as it will make the bag less effective.

Load your bag with pertinent items. You can place stones, herbs, amulets along with personal items signaling your intentions.

Use obsidian arrowheads, basil, lodestone, and a protective amulet for protection.

Fill your bag with three-leaf clover, lucky coins, a rabbit foot, and dried John the Conqueror for good luck.

For wealth and success, keep a lodestone together with a John the Conqueror root, tumbled tiger eye crystals, and a selenite stick.

To attract love, place inside your bag rosehip and magnetized sand with rose quartz heart crystals and dried petals together with a piece of paper containing a love declaration.

Finally, place dried poke root alongside an alligator claw, moss agate crystal, and magnetized salt inside your bag for lifting or crossing a jinx.

When you're done placing all the elements you need inside your bag, the next thing you should do is bless your bag. Do this by blowing into the bag's opening and saying a prayer of blessing: "With my breath, I bless you, just as the Lord breathed into all creatures and gave life to all of us." Draw the cord tight next to secure the bag and its content. Anoint your bag with fix dots or sprays of magic oil. Place a dot on each corner and one right at the center.

Hold your bag and say "I bless you and set you a purpose (state your purpose), and I bind you and give you strength for success."

Afterward, you need to fix your purpose using a magic candle. Write your purpose on a magic candle and impale it with nine pins. Be sure to insert the last pin through the wick just before lighting it and stating your intention once again.

Give your mojo bag a name and make it the physical body of your spiritual ally. Hoodoo practitioners don't treat their bags as merely physical, inanimate tools. Your mojo bag is now a part of you. Naming it will help you associate an energy and personality with it.

How Long Does a Mojo Bag Retain Its Power?

Mojo bags retain their power for at least a year. To keep your bag working, be sure to secure it so that only you, the owner, can see it. If someone else sees or touches your bag, it will render it ineffective.

If you have hard items kept inside the bag, be sure to take them out and clean them once in a while. Soft items like petals and herbs should be replaced when necessary.

It's also important that you feed your bag every week. It's better if you can do it on the same day. Feed your bag with the same oil that was used when you made it. Feed it with incense smoke and prayer too every time you need to call upon it.

Don't allow your bag to get wet or it will lose its efficacy. In case it does get wet, you can revive it using the Rose of Jericho plant, which is also known as the resurrection plant.

There's no need to replace your bag after a year if it is still effective. Different bags will have different strengths, and you will know exactly when to dispose of it and replace it with a new one.

When the time comes that you decide to replace your mojo bag, treat it with respect and honor; give it a proper burial.

Chapter 6: Conjure Work

Conjure work involves an amalgam of influences from various cultures. Hoodoo conjure work is a blend of African beliefs combined with the Protestant base, Germanic, East European cultural influences, and the traditional herbal lore of Native Americans.

It's important to understand that conjure work is merely a spiritual paradigm that is founded in established folk magic of Hoodoo. There are two forms of conjure work, and they are based on wisdom and learning. The first form is based on traditional practices that have been passed down from one generation to another. The more formal stream involves studying intellectual forms of magic.

Traditionally, conjure doctors educated themselves through the study of magical arts from texts containing magical and spiritual knowledge coming from various cultures. The text came in the form of grimoires and other documents containing ancient magic.

Conjuring involves the power of candles and rootwork, as well as the combination of natural elements in forming salves, oils, and powders.

The Right Time to Perform Conjuring

The right time to perform your conjuring whenever you need to. There are no rules regarding when to use it. You can perform them any time you feel you need to and according to your desires and needs. You need to realize, though, that the power of the moon can significantly enhance your work.

The Full Moon

The full moon is seen as a period of abundance and growth. As it begins to wane, it gets small until fading into darkness. If there is a person or thing that you want to banish, you can perform a specific ritual to dispel such a person from your life.

The first thing you need to do is write down that person's or thing's name on a piece of clean paper. Next, get a piece of lemon and slice a hole into it. Cover the lemon with the paper and cover the paper with a piece of red pepper.

Sew the hole using a black thread and pray to your preferred deity or saint to free you from that person before the new moon.

Repeat your prayer for the next fifteen days and watch for signs. Hoodoo will give you signs to help you achieve your goal. You just need to be aware of it and follow the path that is shown to you.

Charging Your Lucky Talisman

Hoodoo doesn't normally depend on the moon for increasing the power of ingredients used in rituals and spells. The ingredients are already powerful enough and only need to be recharged by cleansing them with salt. What the moon does is simply increase the spirituality of mojo bags and other lucky charms. Charging these elements in the new moon is a personal experience and is not meant to be shared with others.

The moon signals the perfect time for rituals. As humans, we are affected by the power of the moon. However, when conjuring, the power comes from the practitioner and not the moon.

The Powder of Powders

Powerful powders are essential elements that every conjuror has in their bag. These powders can be used in various forms of magic. They can be used to power mojo bags, dress wallets, power love potions, attract love, and repel people from your life. They can also be used to remove jinxes and bring wealth and success.

Aphrodite Powder

The best time to conjure using this powder is during the new moon.

To make this powder, you will need:

- Pomegranate seeds
- Organic cocoa powder
- Dried mango skins
- Dried apple skins
- Hibiscus tea leaves
- Hibiscus petals
- Rose petals
- Chamomile tea leaves
- Passionflower essential oil

Use a pestle and mortar to grind all these items together until they form a very fine powder. Ass a few drops of passionflower essential oil and store the final product in a glass bottle.

The Wild West Powder for Crossing or Banishing

The best time to conjure using this powder is during the waning moon.

To make this powder, you will need:

- 3 black cloves
- Onion powder
- Red cayenne powder
- Cumin seeds

- Fresh paprika
- Ground black pepper
- Red hot chili oil

Blend the ingredients together using a small blender. You can also grind the items by hand. Store the final product in a sealed container, ensuring that you wash your hands when handling it.

Hard Cash Powder

The best time to use this is when the full moon happens on a Thursday and the date has a 7 or 9 in it. This powder can be used to attract money and wealth and when you want to increase your chances when gambling.

To make this powder, you will need:

- Cloves
- Chamomile tea leaves
- Fresh ginger
- Dried leaves from a potentilla plant
- Dried nutmeg
- Fresh mint
- A four-leaf clover
- Lavender essential oil.

72

Grind all ingredients together and add a few drops of essential oil before storing in a glass bottle.

Algiers Powder

This powder is used to dust the body and attract romance. It is best used during a full moon.

To make this powder, you will need:

- Dried rose petals
- Deadnettle leaves
- Orris roots
- Vanilla essential oil

Grind all ingredients and add to base flour.

Dream Powder

Use when you want to have prophetic dreams and build a connection to the spirits during sleep. This is best used during a waxing moon.

To make this powder, you will need:

- Cinnamon powder
- Cardamom seeds
- Coriander seeds
- Licorice tea leaves
- Ginger

Grind all ingredients and add to a base flour. Sprinkle the powder onto your pillowcases and bed sheets before going to sleep.

Jinx Removal Powder

The best time to conjure using this powder is during a waning moon.

To make this powder, you will need:

- Dried wintergreen leaves
- Chamomile tea leaves
- Fresh mint leaves
- Citric essential oil

Grind the ingredients together into a paste and add to either a rice flour or cornstarch base.

Controlling Powder

Use this when you want to gain control over others.

To make this powder, you will need:

- Epsom salts
- Magnetic sand
- Dried saltpeter
- Myrrh

Mix all ingredients and add to a base flour.

Cascarilla Powder

This can be used to create a circle of protection. It can cleanse and protect your home when added to a floor wash. You will only need eggshells for this powder. Clean the eggshells and dry them thoroughly before grinding to a fine powder.

Oils

Conjure Oil

This is an all-purpose oil that is used for bringing more power to your conjuring work.

You can use it to enhance your experience and manifest your desires.

To make this oil, you will need:

- Equal parts lotus scented oil
- Equal parts Frankincense
- Equal parts Sandalwood

Mix all three ingredients and store the product in a glass bottle.

Good luck Oil

You will need a base carrier oil from jojoba oil to create good luck oil. Once you have a base oil, you can add to it the following:

- 3 drops of cinnamon oil
- 15 drops of essential lavender oil
- 20 drops of gaultheria oil

To make the oil more money-oriented, you can also add vetiver oil and ginger.

Confusion Oil

This oil is used for making your enemies fight each other.

To make this oil, you will need:

- 1 equal part patchouli oil and 1 equal part chili pepper oil

Add the following ingredients to the oil mixture:

- Blackened peppers (bell, red, green, chili)
- Grains of paradise
- Poppy seeds
- Mustard seeds

You can also add dried vitamin E to strengthen the oil.

Van Van Oil

This one is a classic, with its ingredients having been passed down for many generations. Some of the ingredients may be difficult to obtain, but their absence won't affect the potency of the oil that much.

To create this oil, you will need:

- 2 drops of palmarosa oil

- 16 drops of lemongrass oil
- 32 drops of citronella oil

This is your base oil to which you can further add other ingredients. For instance, you can add essential oils or even dried herbs. However, always remember to dilute the solution using a clean carrier oil when using it.

Other Types of Conjuring

Hoodoo practitioners do not claim to know better than professional medical doctors. At the same time, they understand that some natural substances work as medical treatments for certain conditions.

Headache Salve

To make this salve, you will need:

- 1 cup of light organic oil (sesame oil or sunflower oil)
- 1/2 oz pure beeswax
- White sage
- Lavender
- Eucalyptus
- Vitamin E (liquid)

- Strainer

The ingredients here can be dried or fresh, and it's up to you how much of each you wish to add. Try an ounce each first and make adjustments along the way.

Add all the herbs to a casserole dish and cover them with the oil. Bake the mixture at 180 degrees for 3 hours and allow to cool for 30 minutes afterwards. Remove the herbs and squeeze out the excess liquid using a straining cloth.

Add the herbal infused oil in a stainless-steel pot and let the liquid simmer in low flame for about 10 minutes before adding vitamin E.

Add beeswax to the mixture and continue to heat until the liquid has melted.

Remove the pot and allow it to rest for 5 minutes. Right before the mixture sets, decant it into separate bottles before leaving it to set. Once the salve has cooled and thickened, cover the bottle containers. Use the salve to relieve headaches, spreading a smudge on your temples or forehead.

Wasps Nest Conjuring

A dead wasp's nest can be used for conjuring. If you happen to find one, don't throw it away. To make a wasps nest conjuring, grind the nest and incorporate the powder into your hex or banishing powders.

Hoodoo practitioners believe that wasp nests contain powerful protective powers, as well as the teachings of Treemonisha known as the dirt dauber nest.

Mix some of the ground nest with warm water and goofer dust to create a protective mixture. If you want to create a mixture that allows you to infiltrate the life of another person, wasp nest is an essential ingredient.

Enhancing Your Conjure Work

Spiritual workers understand and recognize the power of words and speech. They understand how words can have the ability to enhance the power of intentions. The Holy Scriptures, in particular, along with prayers, is considered the most powerful form of incantation that can bring strength to the spirit.

Hoodoo places an importance to the Bible as it is packed with useful information that relates with the values of Hoodoo practices.

Important Psalms Use for Strengthening Conjure Work

Psalm 51 This Psalm is used for cleansing and is often used with healing baths. It's a powerful passage containing incantations asking for the washing away of iniquities and sins. Use this Psalm if you feel the need to restore your faith or seek salvation.

Psalm 64 This Psalm is primarily used for protection. It appeals to God to protect one from people with evil intentions. Recite it whenever you feel that you are being threatened or when you want to confront those who are oppressing you.

Psalm 78 This Psalm perfectly mirrors Hoodoo beliefs. It encourages one to pass on their powers and learn from those who have taught them. Use it when you need to

strengthen your psychic abilities or recharge
your talisman.

Psalm 29 This is a cleansing Psalm used to
provide protection for property. It describes
how the Lord struck the land with lightning
and how he cleansed the desert. Use this
passage to deep cleanse your home and
get rid of all negative energies.

Psalm 65 This is referred to as the
gambler's psalm. Use it if you need extra
luck when you are about to gamble. It
should amplify your intentions and help you
attract wealth.

Chapter 7: The Use of Candle Magic

Candles have long been used in religious and spiritual practices. Egyptians have used them for millennia. The Romans also used them in their ceremonies. Buddhists, too, used candles by coating reeds with animal fat.

Early Hoodoo workers have often been depicted as having used candles in their work, but in reality, the slaves who practiced Hoodoo didn't have access to candles. For one, they were too expensive and can only be found in the house of the rich.

Soon after their freedom, former slaves traveled and formed communities. They then marketed candles as a key part of Hoodoo practice. In the 1940s, a series of booklets were published encouraging the use of various types of candles for Hoodoo work. Today, candle magic is popular among beginners.

The Meaning of Candle Colors

Early Hoodoo practitioners didn't recognize the power behind the different colors the candles represented. The two main colors they worked with were black and white, each representing evil and good respectively. As modern Hoodoo began to evolve, so did the beliefs and practices.

Other cultures teach that the color of the candle creates spiritual connections and vibrations, although that's not the case with Hoodoo. The power and magic come not from the candles themselves but from the intent. Nevertheless, some Hoodoo practitioners used colored candles, but mainly to remind themselves of their intent so as not to be distracted.

White Candles These are used for healings and blessings. White candles were the original candles used in traditional Hoodoo.

Black Candles These are used for placing hexes or protecting individuals.

Red Candles These candles represent blood. Blood is the life force of every living creature, making red candles a powerful force as well. These candles form the intentions regarding love and romance and also represent audacity and boldness.

Pink Candles Pink candles are used to focus intentions on domestic affairs. The color represents respect and togetherness between family members. It is also used for healing wounds in the spirit and bringing to life positive energies in the soul.

Blue Candles These candles are burned to bring joy. The color blue signifies peace and harmony and is used to bring peace to households.

Gold Candles Gold candles are used for bringing fortune and wealth.

Orange Candles These are for creating doorways and eliminating blockages. They are used for creating paths for success and enhance mental clarity.

Yellow Candles These candles signify change and fortune. They are used to create situations that can transform the life of the person involved.

Green Candles Green means material gain. Green candles aid magic that is directed toward business matters and help one boost their finances.

Silver and Gray Candles Both candles are helpful when you're casting spells for protection. Burn them to help relieve pain connected to loss and grief.

Purple Candles These represent mastery. Use this candle if you want to enhance your magic while casting an intention of gaining control over others.

Brown Candles These are burned to ensure success in legal matters.

Hoodoo Candle Terminology

Here's a list of candle terminology used in the practice of Hoodoo:

Dressed Candles When dressing candles, practitioners use ingredients for guiding the spirits to their intentions. Ideally, you would select a candle that signals your intention, and then apply oil and roots to strengthen your magic. Whenever you need to attract protection, for instance, you would use a gray candle and cover it with protective oil. You can also mix different types of oil to further enhance your candle.

It's important not to overload your candle with oil, as it may set it on fire. Dress your candle with about four to five drops of oil.

Fixed Candles Fixed candles are similar to dressed candles, only that they are prepared by other people. These candles have been loaded with herbs and oils following intense prayer. They are also loaded with intent.

Loaded Candles These candles are ones that have been carved into and then filled with herbs, roots, and oils. You can make your own loaded candle that suits your intentions or buy one that has been pre-prepared.

Carved Candles Carving a candle is used to direct magic to a particular person or object. You can carve the name of a person and direct your magic toward them. Generic symbols represent how you want your magic to function. The eye symbol, for instance, means protection.

Rolled Candles Rolled candles are candles rolled in oil and herbs. They look impressive but can be dangerous as the herbs can influence how the candle burns. Some elements can fall off and cause fire.

Keep in mind that all types of candles used in Hoodoo are potential fire hazards and should be handled with care. Use encased candles if you can since they are safer and are less likely to catch fire.

Figure Candles

Form candles or effigy candles are not part of traditional Hoodoo, just like colored candles. They are quite a new concept and are not meant to represent spirits or human figures, but are used to remind a practitioner of their intent.

Some people feel that novelty-shaped candles only bring Hoodoo into disrepute. Others believe they can enhance rituals. The best way for a Hoodoo practitioner to decide is to look at the candle and decide for themselves what the candle means.

Skull Candles These candles represent the mind and are often used to infiltrate thoughts and control how you want another person to behave. The color of the candle is related to the intention of the practitioner; white skulls are especially effective for easing grief for those who are mourning.

Devil Candles Also known as Satan candles, these candles are placed in doors and windows to banish evil spirits from the home.

Seven Knob Candles These are powerful candles with seven indentations. They are meant to burn over seven days; you can use them to wish for one thing for a period of seven days or wish for seven different things at once.

Baphomet Sabbatical Goat Goat represents power and force, and this candle is use to coerce other people in non-sexual matters. Burn these candles whenever you want to dominate other people's thoughts.

Cat-Shaped Candles Cats are associated with good luck and good fortune. Burn these candles to attract luck.

Money Pyramid Candle These candles represent power and wealth and are usually decorated with an all-seeing eye. They help protect possessions and the home from damage and theft.
Marriage Pyramid Candle This is a candle with the image of a loving couple embracing. It is used to enhance love and romance.

How to Read Candle Burning

The interpretation of the meaning of a candle's flame is subjective. It can mean different things depending on the material used on both the candle and its wick. To master the art of candle reading, you need to ensure that you purchase your candle from the same source every time, so that the flame is consistent.

You should make your candles yourself as much as possible to know exactly what you are getting.

Hoodoo will serve as your guide to the result it believes that you deserve. If you use a badly made candle and get a message that sends you to a different path, then simply accept that the outcome was meant to be. As your work improves, interpretation of signs will become second nature to you.

The Meaning Behind Candle Flames

There are so many different ways a candle can burn, and each will have its own meaning. When burning your magic candles, ensure that the flame burns true and is not influenced by drafts.

- A steady upward flame means that everything is going well.

- A flame that jumps means that someone wants to contact you desperately. This isn't necessarily negative and could mean that the spirits are encouraging you for your work.
- When the flame dances or is flickering from side to side in a rhythmic manner, it means that your energies are going wild. The flame is telling you to refocus and get rid of distractions.
- A shrinking flame means there is a lack of energy. When this happens, it means you are taking longer to reach your desires and goals.
- A heightened flame offers mixed messages. It could mean that your work will be completed a lot faster, but it could also indicate the results of your work will be short-lived.
- A blue flame normally means you are on the right track and that your magic has a higher chance of succeeding.
- A green flame indicates wealth. This doesn't always mean money, but that whatever you desire will come in abundance.

- White smoke is a good sign and means that you are successful in your work.
- Black smoke signals opposition. Someone is working against you, and you need to abandon your work and cast a road opener or blockage spell before resuming with your current intention.

How to Read Candle Wax

Reading candle wax in Hoodoo is called ceromancy. It is performed by interpreting how wax runs down a burning candle. If the candle is contained properly and is standing on a level surface, your reading and interpretation will be more precise.

Tears If the candle wax appears like human tears, it could mean that tears will be shed as a result of your work. If the formation stops before the candle runs out, it means the grief will be temporary.

Pinnacles If the wax doesn't reach the bottom of the candle or breaks off, it means someone involved in your spells is trying to hold on to the past. That person may be carrying issues, and this can hinder your work.

The absence of wax dips indicates that you are successful. It means your work has been executed perfectly, and you will be able to guarantee success.

If the wax spreads unevenly like a puddle, it's a sign that your wish has been granted. However, it also means that there are other paths that you will need to take and that your work is not yet over.

Wax running down on a single side means something unusual is going on. It could render your spell incomplete, and it could mean that you have an imbalance in your spirit.

How to Read Wax Puddles

Candle wax should form a shape that is easily recognizable when you're performing certain rituals. For instance, heart-shaped puddles indicate romance, while some shapes can mean that something negative is happening.

Remnants that resemble claws mean that someone is spreading lies and gossip about you. You should repeat your work until you see the wax burning smoothly.

Wax puddles that resemble genitalia means troubled relationships or infidelity.

Wax pillars that aren't natural-looking or look like figures of monsters show that the spell is not successful due to external turbulence. Cast some powder oil to eliminate these negative influences.

Coffin-shaped wax puddles mean that your jinx or hex spells have been successful, and whatever threat there is against you has been defeated.

Chapter 8: Rootwork

Slaves were stripped of their freedom and had little to no control over their lives. However, while the slave masters had their physical bodies, they couldn't have their spirits. The slaves retained control of their spirits and used their imagination to keep their spirits and hopes up, especially during the most difficult times.

A famous personality called High John developed a reputation during the era of slavery for inspiring the slaves with stories of his deeds and how he was able to overcome his master. He is better known as High John the Conqueror, a huge man who used skill and trickery to avoid doing work.

It is said that High John was an African prince who was sold into slavery. Some say he was just a commoner. Regardless of his origin, he was well known for his ability to avoid work. He was a strong man and luck seemed to be always on his side. He was known for being able to outsmart his opponents even though he would play dumb.

High John was associated with Ipomea Jalapa, the most powerful root often found inside a Hoodoo worker's bag of magic. Most practitioners would carry High John Root to remove obstacles and overcome their enemies. Placing it inside a green mojo bag magnifies its lucky element. It will then help attract wealth to the carrier.

Popular Roots and Herbs in Hoodoo

Angelica Root This is also known as Archangel root. When you sprinkle dried Angelica roots in the four corners of your house, it will protect your home from evil. Use this root to enhance work aimed at purification or the uncrossing of hexes. Moreover, this root will help bring back lost romance.

Bats Head Root Also known as ling nut, horny bulls head, and Devil pod, bats head root strangely resembles the head of a devil. Use it whenever you want your wishes to come true and remove any obstacle in the way.

Blood Rot Root This root can be used for multiple purposes. It can help fix family and marital disputes and improve sex life at the same time. Burning It during a ritual can stop another person from taking your lover. You can also place it by the window to attract new partners.

Calamus Root Burn this root while performing other types of work to enhance the potency of the original spell. This is a dominating root and can increase the strength of your work in any situation.

Devils Shoestring Root This root can be used to change your luck when looking for a new job. It can also help you at your current workplace. Carry it when you're seeking employment or when you wish to gain control over the opposite sex.

Fennel Hang this in your home or workplace to ward off evil spirits and negative energies. It works especially well with female practitioners and can attract money and wealth for them.

Hazel This is used to make amulets for fertility. Hang some twigs on your windows to keep lightning strikes away.

Lavender This herb brings harmony and sexual satisfaction to couples who are experiencing problems in the bedroom. It is sometimes used to prevent domestic abuse; rub it on the victim, and it will serve as some sort of shield.

Magnolia The buds from this flower can be used by males to attract females. It can also be used to elicit fidelity and keep partners from looking for other lovers.

Nutmeg This is a lucky herb and is a favorite of gamblers. It can be used to attract wealth and luck and is a sign of prosperity.

Galangal Root Also known as the Chewing John root, this root is a powerful protection root that is chewed while casting reverse hex spells. The remains are spitted out to dispel hex spells from your life. If you are facing a court case, burn Galangal root two weeks before the date of the hearing for success. You can also use this root to attract wealth. Just wrap money around it, and it will do its job.

Ginger Hoodoo considers ginger as one of its most important and versatile roots. It is used for promoting self-confidence, sensuality, and prosperity. Use ginger to increase the potency of your rootwork and speed up its outcome.

Queen Elizabeth Root This is an influential root that can be used for conjuring for love and sex. It is also known as orris root, and can attract the opposite sex and increase the potential for long-term romance. It is sprinkled on the sheets before lovemaking and is used to strengthen marriage and promote fertility.

Hyssop This is a cleansing herb that has been used for a very long time. It is a powerful herb for cleansing the home and getting rid of hexes.

Five Finger Grass This herb is also known as cinquefoil. It is used for attracting money and success. When you bathe in water infused by a solution of five finger grass, you will be able to get rid of even the most stubborn of jinxes.

Licorice Root Licorice can be used when you want to change the mind of another person or influence their thinking.

Mugwort Artemisia vulgaris or mugwort is a special root used for cleaning magical tools like talismans and crystals. It has the power to remove negativity and restore the energy and potency of such tools.

Parsley In Hoodoo, parsley is used to promote peace and calm in the family. It can also be used to guard food against contamination. More importantly, it is used to aid healing following surgery or illness.

Pepper Tree Pepper tree is a powerful herb used for protection. It has healing properties, too, and can help in the recovery of people who have gone through surgery.

Thyme This herb helps in boosting psyching powers and purifying rootwork. It can help you gain knowledge and the courage to press on with your work.

Witch Hazel Bark An item brought by the Native Americans to Hoodoo, this is used to heal skin and oral conditions. When used in rootwork, it can encourage chastity and reduce passion. Having this bark in your possession when you're grieving can also help reduce grief.

Creating Talismans and Amulets Using Herbs and Roots

A Talisman and amulet are not the same thing. The former is a man-made object that is charged with power. They can be crafted using various materials and are usually worn around the neck or on the fingers as a ring. They can also be decorated with natural items, such as stones or crystals.

The latter, on the other hand, is a natural object that can be consecrated or blessed to be used for conjuring or magic. Amulets can be charged with intention depending on what the user requires.

How to Create an Amulet

Amulets are often made of durable material, such as stones or gemstones. Hag stone is one of the most common elements used for creating one. A hag stone is a stone with holes caused naturally by running water.

The shape of the stone you choose suggests what its potential power will be. For instance, a heart-shaped stone is ideal for love spells. On the other hand, a stone resembling a dagger can be used for protection. Make your amulet wearable by using natural fibers or cords so that you can wear it around your neck or wrist.

Use water with sacred salt to cleanse and consecrate your amulet. This will remove any negative energy or impurities from the amulet. Let it dry naturally and pass it through the burning smoke of selected herbs until you feel that it is already charged.

Charging an amulet may involve calling on to your preferred deities to protect you and bestow you with strength and love.

How to Create a Talisman

To create a talisman, you first need to choose a central object as your focus. This can be a pendant or ring that you own. Coins, keys, and similar metal objects can be used to further enhance the appearance of your talisman.

Once you've chosen an object, determine what the purpose of your talisman will be.

Are you going to use it for protection? Will you be using it to attract love? Choose the best time of the month to work on your talisman to increase its strength. Check the lunar cycles to find out which time is the best to start crafting it.

To make your talisman wearable, you can use leather straps that enable you to wear the talisman around your neck or waist. Use roots and herbs to create an infusion to bless your talisman. Sprinkle the item with a few drops every day, making sure that it is stored in a safe place.

Charge the talisman with energy from your inner being, allowing the strength of your intentions to penetrate the piece until it vibrates with your spirit.

Summon your favorite spirits or deities to bless the item and protect your work.

You can also cast a simple grounding spell on the talisman if you have excess energy. You can do this by burning sandalwood and sage on a slate disc and lighting a white candle on top of any natural stone. Connect to the flame of the candle by sitting in front of it and starting at it as the flame dances.

Take deep breaths as you watch the flame and visualize roots growing from your arms and legs.

Visualize the roots burrowing deep into the ground and feel yourself connecting with the earth and the cosmos. Use the roots to channel all your fears and anxieties and feel them disappearing into the depths of the earth. Keep focusing on your breath as you feel all the negative energies go away.

How To Use Roots and Magic Herbs in Spell Work

- Rolling candles in dried herbs and roots will help the candle burn more effectively.
- Burn dried roots and herbs on slate disks or charcoal.
- Use an incense
- Sturdier herbs can be directly burned. Flammable herbs, such as rosemary, sage, Italian cypress, and eucalyptus must be handled with care.
- Use roots and herbs to make tinctures to make their power last for months at a time.

Chapter 9: Hoodoo Divination

Divination used to be reserved for professional sightseers and for those who had the gift of telling other people's fortunes. Non-practitioners would seek the help of these people and ask them to perform readings on their behalf. As Hoodoo became more popular, practitioners realized they could only perform rituals but not have any means of purchasing tarot cards, crystals, and other accessories.

As a result, they used household objects as tools for divination rites. They used ordinary cards instead of tarot cards and common objects instead of ivory for cleromancy.

Cartomancy

Cartomancy is divination using a deck of cards. Gypsies used ordinary cards to tell the future, with the four suits representing the four elements: earth, wind, fire, and water. Each suit of cards contains a hierarchy that represents leaders and ordinary subjects. The King and Queen are served by their pages, and the rest are the subjects who serve them.

Card Spreads

This term describes how the cards are dealt and what one can expect from the combinations.

Single cards are used to get quick answers to direct questions.
Three-card spreads are used for signifying the past, preset, and future.
Nine-card spreads work similarly to a three-card spread but with added information.
The Gypsy Spider Web is made up of 21 individual cards in three rows of seven and involves more detailed information about the past, present, and future.

The Meaning Behind the Cards

The Suits

Hearts: Hearts represent fire and are connected to the home and affairs relating to emotions.

Diamonds: Diamonds represent the wind and are connected to affairs related to work.

Clubs: Clubs represent the earth and relate to matters on money and finances.

Spades: Spades represent water and are related to roadblocks and obstacles that can cause life problems.

The Individual Cards

King: The King is a sage man who gives excellent advice

Queen: The Queen is a lady with light hair

Jack: The Jack is a younger person with blonde hair

Ten: Ten represents joy and happiness

Nine: Nine means your hopes and wishes will come true

Eight: Eight means your social life will improve

Seven: Seven means treachery and broken promises

Six: Six means good fortune and serendipity

Five: Five represents envious people

Four: Four means a change of environment or maybe marriage in the future
Three: Three means you have to slow down and remain vigilant
Two: Two represents a solid relationship, wealth, and success
Ace: The Ace represents love, joy, and a new beginning

DIAMONDS

King A powerful yet stubborn and obstinate man with light hair
Queen A flirtatious woman who loves to gossip
Jack A younger person with light hair who is often the black sheep of the family
Ten Ten represents a new environment, as well as success and positive changes
Nine Nine represents news regarding money and career
Eight Eight represents maturity in marriage, travel in a cold environment, and financial changes
Seven Seven represents work-related matters, as well as unexpected gifts
Six Six represents issues related to second marriages

Five Five represents a happy family life and career success
Four Four represents money, as well as unexpected legacies or bequests
Three Three represents legal issues, particularly relating to family
Two Two represents unconventional love affairs
Ace Ace represents correspondence related to financial matters

CLUBS

King A kind and loving man with dark hair
Queen An attractive and confident older woman with dark hair
Jack A reliable younger friend with dark hair
Ten Represents luck, foreign travel, and financial news
Nine Represents new romantic relationships
Eight Represents marriage and relationship problems
Seven Means that you have to be careful of the Work? opposite gender; also means success and wealth

Six Means you have to seek help with financial matters; also means you will succeed in business

Five Represents new friends and a happy marriage

Four Means bad times are coming, and you will encounter dishonesty and betrayal

Three Represents marriage to a wealthy person or financial assistance from your spouse

Two Represents lies and backstabbing

Ace Represents news regarding finances, health, happiness, and wisdom

SPADES

King A powerful, self-confident man with jet black hair

Queen An immoral and deceitful widow with dark hair

Jack A younger man with questionable reputation but is immature and well-meaning

Ten Represents bad luck and worries

Nine Represents general misfortune or even death

Eight Represents cancellation of plans and disputes in the family and at work

Seven Represents lost friendships

Six Represents small triumphs that result in major changes

Five Represents outside influences that disrupt the family

Four Represents bad health and financial problems

Three Represents infidelity

Two Represents difficult decisions regarding partnerships

Ace Represents death, arguments, and obsessions

Remember that some people use jokers in their decks. In cartomancy, a joker means new beginnings or taking risks.

How to Shuffle Your Deck

There's no single style of shuffling a deck of cards for cartomancy. Shuffling quickly means you are looking for answers to questions as quickly as possible. Shuffling a little longer means you are interested in a wide spectrum of reading.

Seekers should be asked to cut the deck into multiple piles. Those who cut shallow may be reluctant to trust the advice they will receive, while those who cut deep are confident in the results the reader will give them.

Gifted readers rely on a mix of their knowledge and intuition. The spread is just the beginning of the journey. The more you practice, the better results you will receive.

Augury

Augury is a form of divination that involves reading signs and omens in telling the future. The practice goes as far back as the Ancient Egyptian times, although formal augury was thought to have originated in Rome.

The term is derived from the Latin *auspicium* and *auspex*, which means "looking at birds." This means the first practitioners of this divination observed the movement of birds to get results.

The most powerful first step you can take in practicing this form of divination is to let the birds come to you. Wild birds visiting means you are receiving a message from the divine world.

Types of Birds and Their Meaning

Ravens and Crows

Black birds like ravens and crows are often associated with death or bad luck. Perhaps it's because of their color. Regardless, such misconceptions must be ignored when practicing Hoodoo. In reality, these black birds are a harbinger of well-meaning messages. They even bring good luck and protection.

Hawks

Hawks represent foresightedness. They have superior vision and signifies that you need to be more aware of your surroundings and view the bigger picture with careful consideration and wisdom.

Owls

Owls are considered psychopomps in some cultures. They are spirits or creatures sent to earth to guide a soul to heaven. In Hoodoo augury, owls are seen as a sign that someone is going to die. Native Americans even believe that these birds are sent by evil spirits to spy on humans.

Hummingbirds

These may be small birds, but they are strong and beautiful, always a joy to behold. The appearance of a hummingbird means that the spirits are sending you a message of love and joy. The way these birds dance is simply amazing, and it is nature's way of showing you what harmony looks like.

Doves

Doves have always been seen as a sign of good intentions and hope. Some, however, see them as a symbol of death. That said, white birds are not always a positive sign.

How many birds there are and how they are
behaving should help guide you in
interpreting what message they bring. A
single bird is usually a message telling you
to recharge your psychic abilities. Pairs
often signify romans, while multiple birds
emphasize the strength of belief.

You should also observe whether the birds
are flying or are acting in an unusual
manner. Some birds behave abnormally to
warn of physical danger, such as a storm,
fire, or earthquake.

Are the birds flying toward the South or the
East? South represents love and passion,
while East indicates a place of salvation or
paradise. West has two meanings. It could
mean darkness or divine blessing and
liberation. North, on the other hand, means
performance.

Cleromancy

Cleromancy is the ancient art of divination by means of casting lots. Bones were traditionally used for this practice, but you can use all kinds of items to perform cleromancy, whether stones, shells, dice, or even dominos.

Curing Bones

If you're going to use bones for cleromancy, use chicken or turkey bones. Cure them first by boiling some water in a pot for 20 minutes. Ensure that the flesh has been completely stripped off before taking the bones out and allowing them to cool. Next, fill a plastic container with 1/2 gallon of water and 1/4 cup of bleach. Soak the bones in this mixture for an hour.

Afterwards, you can bless the bones with some sage smudging or anoint them with oil while placed in sacred salt.

Using The Bones

Yes/No Method

Take a bone and ask a direct question.
Drop the bone onto a table or altar, and if
the bone lies vertically, the answer is no. If
the bone lies horizontally, the answer is yes.

Scrying

Scrying involves interpreting the images
formed by the bone. Take several bones
and drop them on a surface from a height of
one foot. Concentrate on the image made
by the bones and consider what the image
is trying to tell you.

Oneiromancy

Oneiromancy is the art of divination through
the interpretation of dreams. The following
are common dreams and what they mean.

Driving

Vehicles represent the soul. When you
dream of driving, it means your life is going
through changes. If you are the passenger,
it could mean that you need to take charge
of your decisions.

Flying

This means you are ready to make advancements in your life. You are being directed to new beginnings.

Teeth Falling Out

Most people interpret this as death, but more symbolically, it represents a loss of vitality. It's a sign that you need to take care of yourself for your energy levels to increase again.

Spiders

Arachnids in your dream means there's an authoritative figure who is causing you stress. This could be an issue at home or at work.

Climbing Mountains

Dreaming of climbing mountains means you
are striving for advancement and self-
improvement. The spirits might be telling
you to start believing in yourself.

Chapter 10: Hoodoo Spells for Love and Luck

Love spells are a great way to strengthen relationships by restoring lost affection. However, if a relationship is falling apart, it may be destined to fail, and no amount of Hoodoo spells will save it. In most cases, you can cast spells to help you and your partner get through difficult times in your relationship, especially if the problem isn't too serious.

Create a Safe Space

Before casting a love spell, ensure that you and your partner are mentally and physically in a safe space. Being surrounded with positive energy will help your relationship become more receptive to the spell.

There are deities associated with love that you can ask help from, including Aphrodite and Cernunnos.

Remember to choose your spell carefully, and understand that it often comes with consequences. Follow the instructions carefully and study what the outcomes will be.

Quick Conciliation Spell

This spell is used to bring two people back together following an argument.

You will need a note with the handwritten words of Psalm 32 on it, a pink tapered candle, 8 tacks, a jar of honey, a piece of slate, and a pin or needle.

To begin the spell, take the note and turn it over, writing the name of the other person on the space. Take a pin or needle and carve the name of that person into the candle three times.

Next, stand the candle on the piece of slate, surrounding the base with the tacks. Cover the tacks with honey. This will "sweeten" the pain of the separation. Burn the candle for three days straight while reciting Psalm 32. Your spell will be cast after the third day.

Honey Jar Spell

This spell is good for relationships that have gone boring. If you want to restore feelings of love and romance, then use this spell.

For this, you will need a pen and paper, a piece of slate, pink or red candles, herbs and roots that you prefer, such as rose petals and magnolia, attraction oil or powder, and a jar with honey inside.

You first need to write the name of the other person on the piece of paper three times. Next, rotate the paper and write your name the same number of times so that it forms a block, overlapping the name of your partner. Encircle the block with words of love and phrases like "return to me" or "love me" without lifting the pen.

Add herbs and oils to the paper and other personal items of your choice. You can even add bodily fluids or strands of hair to enhance it. Afterwards, charge the jar with roots, herbs, and other items associated with romance.

Place the paper into the honey jar and recite the words, "This honey is sweet to me just like (say the name of your partner) will be sweet and loving to me."

Lick any honey from your hands and repeat the ritual two more times. Close the jar and store it in a cool place.

Place the candle on the slate and anoint it using the honey from the jar. Light the candle and ask help from your favorite spirits and deities. Repeat this ritual for three days, and your spell will be cast.

Getting Rid of an Unwanted Lover

This spell is for getting rid of a lover or breaking up a couple who are not supposed to be together. For this spell, you will need a red rose, a paper with the names of the person you want to get rid of or the couple involved, four pieces of nails, and a hammer.

Start by dressing the piece of paper with banishing oils or herbs, such as sage, pepper, or garlic. Fold the paper so that it can be enfolded into the rose petals. Next, find a dead tree and nail the paper/rose combination with the four nails. Beat the flower and destroy it. Walk home without looking back, and your spell is cast.

A Spell to Attract New Love

This spell works for both sexes and is meant for attracting love and tenderness. It attracts a natural form of love and doesn't force someone to love you. For this spell, you will need an altar or decorated table, a white marriage candle, and a white rose bush's thorn.

Perform the spell by first decorating the altar or table with objects that symbolize you and the person you love. These can be clothing items, pictures, or mementos. Take the thorn of the rose bush and inscribe the candle with the phrase, "Come to me, my love" and the name of the person you are attracting. Do this three times.

Burn the candle on the altar and visualize the person coming toward you with loving intentions.

After the candle has burned down completely, collect the wax puddle and the rest of the items from the altar and store them.

Luck Spells

This time, let's focus on spells that bring luck and wealth. It's very important that you create the right space for using luck and wealth spells. Fortune will come to you when you perform these spells, but your spells will be even more powerful if you take time to create the right space to perform them.

Setting Up Your Altar

An altar doesn't need to be complicated for it to work. It could be as simple as a table set up in one of the rooms in your home. The most important thing to remember is that this altar should only be used for magic work and spells.

You can personalize your altar and make it a representation of what you believe. You can decorate it with different colored candles or coverings to indicate your intentions as you do your magic.

Green is the color to utilize when performing spells to attract luck and wealth. Cover the altar with a green cloth or use green candles for your spells to be more effective.

In addition, charge your altar with the four elements by placing a jar filled with sand to the north, a bowl filled with water to the west, an incense stick to the east, and a green candle to the south.

You can also charge your altar with lucky gods and goddesses. Ganesh, for instance, is an Indian god representing prosperity and achievements. Mahakala, is also a god of luck, and so is the Egyptian god Bes.

Good Luck Spell

For a basic good luck spell, you will need three green candles, three pieces of acorn, and an incense. To perform the spell, place the three candles to form a triangle and place a piece of acorn at each corner of the triangle. Light the candles and incense together and recite this prayer: "Lady luck and all her handmaidens, I ask for your help. Give me the strength of a bear and the luck of a rabbit. I summon the four elements to bless my work. Bring me health and wealth, and bring luck to all that I do. So be it."

Take the wax of the candle after it has burned down and wrap it in green silk. Bury it under a fruit-bearing tree, and your spell is cast.

The Money Spell

A simple money spell can be performed over a period of nine days to get successful results. It can be performed any time of the day, but it should be repeated at the same time every time. For this spell, you will need a green and white candle and any prosperity oil, such as eucalyptus, bergamot, or jasmine.

The green candle represents wealth and money while the white represents you. You can inscribe your name on the white candle to maximize the results.

First, you need to charge the candles with your chosen oil and place them on the altar nine inches apart. Next, light both candles and repeat this prayer:

"Money and wealth come to me, in fullness and in plenty three times three. I seek enrichment without harming me. With your help, it will be done. Money, I welcome you three times three."

After this, move both candles an inch closer to each other and extinguish the flames. Repeat this for nine days. On the ninth day, allow the candles to burn completely before wrapping the remains in a white cloth and placing them inside your mojo bag.

Spell to Grow Your Business

You can use this spell if you have a business that doesn't seem to grow no matter how hard you work to improve it. For this spell, you will need a large plate, 1/4 cup of curd, a red mojo bag, fast luck oil, almond oil, a small magnet, seven coins, and one green, red, yellow, and blue candle.

Write the name of your business on a piece of paper and place the paper under the plate. Carve the symbol of the sun on each of the candles and anoint them with the oils. Place the curd on top of the place and arrange the seven coins into the shape of a horseshoe. Take the green candle and place it at the top of the plate, the blue to the left, the yellow to the right, and the red at the bottom.

Position the magnet at the center of the candles and light the green candle.

Pray to the gods of abundance and ask for their aid. Light the yellow candle and continue praying. Do the same with the red and blue candles.

Once the candles have burned down, take the remains of the wax, curd, and coins, and place them inside your mojo bag. Carry them with you all the time. The spell should be reenergized every six months or whenever you feel it necessary. This spell should take effect and help you in growing your business.

Dream Job Spell

Use this spell if you need to change your career and earn more money. For this spell, you will need a piece of pen and paper, peppermint oil, a silver coin, three cloves of garlic, and a green mojo bag.

Write a detailed description of the job you are dreaming of on the paper. Include your salary expectations and job responsibilities you wish to have. Sprinkle the paper with peppermint oil and place the paper inside your mojo bag.

Place the garlic and silver coin inside the bag and repeat this prayer seven times:

"Work and love go hand in hand, bless my life with both, help me find the best for me, and let my career grow."

Lucky Seven's Ritual for Money and Success

This ritual is an example of the connection Hoodoo has with numerology. It's specifically associated with the number seven and how it represents luck and success. For this spell, you will need 8 single dollar bills with 7 as each of their Federal Reserve numbers. You will find this number as part of the two-digit mark on the dollar note indicating which back the note has originated from. Seven refers to Chicago, and it will come with a letter as well.

You will also need one clear quartz crystal, one iron pyrite stone or fool's gold, and one Aventurine quartz.

It's ideal that the bills come to you naturally over a period of time. The power won't work as well if you went to the bank and asked for the bills you need.

Patience is key to this spell. Once you have collected all the bills you need, begin by giving one to a close friend and explaining to them what you wish to achieve. The larger the number of people involved in the ritual, the more powerful the magic will be.

As for the remaining seven dollars, place them on your altar or in a silver money clip. Place the crystal and the rest of the items on top of the bills and leave them to charge for one week or seven days.

As the people in your group gift you with relevant dollar bills, swap them for the ones you have in your original pile. This will inject fresh energy into the ritual, and over time, you will experience more prosperity and wealth.

Conclusion

Hoodoo can be a very powerful tool at the hands of the right person. You have been given the opportunity to learn how to use Hoodoo for attracting love and wealth, as well as protecting yourself against evil people. Be sure to use your powers responsibly and respect the guidelines accompanying the folk magic entrusted to you.

You have the choice to use magic for both good and evil, and you have the potential to use magic to cause pain and distress to others. Always allow your conscience to guide you and lead you to the right path. Instead of harming others, do your best to use magic to bring love and happiness to the world.

www.ingramcontent.com/pod-product-compliance
Lightning Source LLC
Chambersburg PA
CBHW071909120726
48001CB00005B/1671